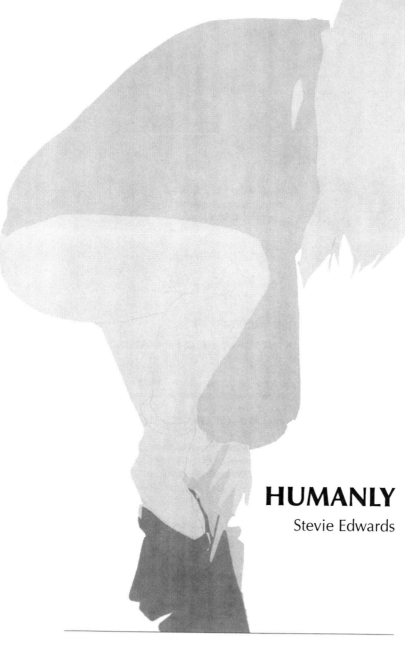

HUMANLY

Stevie Edwards

a division of

SMALL
DOGGIES
PRESS

Portland, Oregon

SMALL DOGGIES PRESS
a division of Small Doggies Omnimedia
smalldoggiesomnimedia.com

Humanly
poetry by Stevie Edwards

SMALL DOGGIES PRESS © 2015
1ST PRINTING.

ISBN 978-0-9848744-8-4

PRINTED IN THE UNITED STATES OF AMERICA
10 · 9 · 8 · 7 · 6 · 5 · 4 · 3 · 2 · 1

Small Doggies trade paperback edition, March 2015
HUMANLY, COPYRIGHT 2015. • ALL RIGHTS RESERVED.

PUBLISHED BY SMALL DOGGIES PRESS, PORTLAND, OR.

Small Doggies Press: WWW.SMALLDOGGIESPRESS.COM
WWW.STEVIETHECLUMSY.COM

Edited by *Carrie Seitzinger*.
Cover Art by *Natasha Law*.
Cover Design by *Olivia Croom*.
Interior Layout by *Olivia Croom*.
Type set in Palatino & **Optima**

Preface to Eating the Night Whole

No answer, but the body still asks as it hinges
toward a new decade of knowing
the mutt it carries, fang and fantasy, is
not a pet that can be put down per se
but an abiding beast that prowls in the too quiet—
What have you done? Lord knows,
I'd sell my dainty left ear to be a painter
of pleasant still-lifes, throw the right one in free.

For the Women of Pink Door

Contents

FANG AND FANTASY

ANCHOR

For a man who has been through bitter experiences and travelled far can enjoy even his sufferings after a time.
—Homer, *The Odyssey* (translated by E.V. Rieu)

——————•◦•——————

"But I don't want to go among mad people," Alice remarked.

"Oh, you can't help that," said the Cat: "We're all mad here. I'm mad. You're mad."

"How do you know I'm mad?" said Alice.

"You must be," said the Cat, "Or you wouldn't have come here."

—Lewis Carroll, *Alice's Adventures in Wonderland*

Dread Clothes

Luck, Luck, Noose

In the dewy brain of morning they haven't been cut down.

The two young men, my college friends, are still
pendulums closing in upon death.

I study the tiny oscillations across my ceiling:
a hypnotist's watch. I am feeling very…
like I have felt those eyes

in my stomach, an un-wanting so boundless
it knows my innards better than any ultrasound.

I can't imagine you like it,
being two tragedies strung up in the same room like this.

Was there ever a time we three creeps sat down
together at Baldwin Hall,
glared in silent, disapproving unison
at overcooked noodles and canned peaches?

I don't think this happened—Josh, John,
gentlemen of this breakneck brigade—

I have brought you here to discuss the rules of dying:
I've been stacking cards for a decade.

Dad taught me to slap the best trick on the ass
of the euchre deck while I tilled the cards in,
hold it there three shuffles,

then wait—one card, two cards, three cards,
let the gem slide in at the four spot.

Stave off the cut with a smile
too wholesome for a cheat.

The first time I tried to slip my outsides
I failed. The second, the third—
wrong stacks of pills I couldn't keep down.

The fourth, a bluff at death. I wanted to keep it:
life, the embarrassment,

even the professor's email ...*You don't know
what day it is. You're confused...*
on a Sunday I thought was Monday,

said I was too ill for fiction,
after having risen from a heaved pool
of my own dark brewing.

Gentlemen, what finally shooed you
out of dread clothes,
into nooses? No,

don't speak to me. I am
cutting old towels, rags to dust the dead skin
from my room.

All you little yous flocking the light fixture.
Oh, I am coming for you, fixing
to shut you up good.

First Move After the Year of Hangings

The former tenant's useless harvest,
a collection of dead
weeds, dried brittle and heaped,
hangs in wait in the attic.
What facet of their form did he love
enough to gather but not to U-Haul
across this small town? Why delight
in such fragility? The ugly, quiet
shattering of epidermis and veins,
the chronic scent of death continuing.
Not that I believe in haunting,
not that I blame him for wanting a world
I can't understand the beauty of—
I just wish he hadn't left the naked stalks
bound together in twine like that,
suspended in dust from the vaulted ceiling:
there are worse things to find
in a windowless room than inanimate
flora. I know I should be grateful
this is all I am charged to cut down today.

Theory of Time

Try this: my bed is covered in Kleenex and late bills.
I am starting to forget stilled frames: where I put
the stamps, the extra cellphone battery, my dead
grandmother's phone number I must have called
a hundred times. It started with 694. I'm afraid
these prescriptions that slow neuron riots edging
my system toward overload have taken away time,
how it used to hover before me or me behind it.
I could at least see and catalogue tiny oscillations
of wing, fist, story, garbage. Broke for memories,
let's invent a room I used to stay in. A good find
for the price, someone had bothered to paint the walls
a shade other than the landlord's eggshell, maybe red
with sloppy trim work around the doorframe—
either unskilled or possessed by the laze that comes
with temporary housing, with no time to nest
before the next life plan reaching out of Tarot cards
and spreadsheets. If I dash numb sky rational
at a rate of Lamictal and wine into tenure track
and vintage suits, at what point do I pass the fragile
center of ghosts in the brain, and is it better?

Fiat Lux

The scientist on YouTube is trying to chart a place
defined by light. Below known waters,
animals glow for each other.
Every day this has happened
while I've steeped espresso on the stovetop
alone, examining the weather
through warped windowpanes.

Naturally, we are destroying this world
in the name of banal luxuries.
How common, the images of carnage:
a net, a small boat trawling the ocean floor,
a shrimp on a cocktail fork, shelled, its shit-vein
extracted by a petite, curved blade
designed to make disembowelment less fuss.

She has developed new instruments
for capturing the spectacular
strange lights on film: a white finger brushes
golden coral, the shy tentacles bray
electric war paint, we think
—the scientist and I—
that it would like to be left alone.

Sometimes, blue neon
is a scream in the dark, sometimes a lure.
I consider the fantastic
vocabularies illuminating deep seas:
I do not think that they sing for me.

I watch as she shuts out the lights,
shakes a jar of plankton to provoke them
into donning their full, frightened glamour.
As the audience waits for bright yelps to emerge,
she jokes that she hopes their silence
is not evidence of death.

To Houdini

There's a theatrics to escaping ruin
that has to be honed.
The world wants to see you struggle
loosening the straitjacket's hold,
chip your teeth on the buckle,
worry your brow, throw your body
violently against water tank walls.
There must be real danger.
Let them bury you,
the unreal weight of the ground
bearing down upon your chest.
I have said that my dreads are like this:
February's drear, new evidence
of roaches, loss after loss
inhuming the living room.
I have never undergone lightless
like you. Disinter yourself
in the full terror of knowing
the dirt ceiling of death.
We are all waiting to clap and gasp
and photograph this miracle
you've been preparing
for us to believe in.

Double Survivor

for Tsutomu Yamaguchi

When nobody would employ your cadaverous frame
except occupying forces;
when your hair fell out for fifteen years
of trying to be new again;
when your burned skin kept burning;
when chickens pecked
a colony of maggots in your stripped skin;
when your daughter found you hideous
in your perpetual bandages;
when nine cancers took your son;
did you curse or thank the recalcitrant drum
daring your body forward
into this world that sanctioned
scarifying your life?
Cataract your eyes.
The strange white flash
that turned your skin inside out, twice,
in two abraded cities,
will be what you are remembered for:
what stole earth from you.

Accident

Ryan jumps out of planes to save
the country, and it's not an accident
to skirt the sky and skid the ground
until he says he almost died
last night. Then it is.

It was an accident to spit
too much butane on the grill coals,
to char my smooth brow
in the flame billow.

The crescent scar: proof
the body tries until it can't.

And he's supposed to keep jumping,
like the ground isn't a hungry casket.

How many tragedies does it take
to turn off all the light bulbs
and slip into a shadow more suitable
for unliving in?

The answer: if you have to ask,
there is still more to lose.

And he's supposed to keep jumping.

For the Handsome Academic Nursing a Local IPA, Explaining How Heroin Isn't Any Worse Than Drinking

She had to tell the nurse that vein wouldn't take anymore.
She, half a country, a half-decade, a first book away
from a wreckage of need I never knew her in or apart from.
She still lives like a junky, one friend says
in concerned judgment. I think this means drifting
without a lease or cleaning supplies.

In this story it's July in mid-gentrification Logan Square,
and hipsters are exploding her lawn with fireworks
smuggled effortlessly into the city from Indiana.

She's wearing a structured red dress that shows off
her freckled shoulders. It is this night
I first consider how similar our bodies are:
born within a year of each other
with hips and blood and waists, petite little things.
I want to hold her and sway to living
musicians strumming and yelping to varying degrees
of atonal competence. I want to stay in this
story where nobody gets hurt.

Because I always avert my gaze from the places
I expect to see scars, I remember best
her blue eyes, the red dress, her thick calves:
I won't tell you what's happened since.

The Devil I Know

It's 4:30 PM in Ithaca on a Saturday,
nearly Christmas, and all through the apartment
the dense stench of a bender heaved
until dry, until *I swear to God there's nothing
left inside me,* until blood—
a gory pool drooled on the fitted sheet,
on the Michael Kors blouse I never took off,
the floral comforter, more on the floor.
Time to play detective again.
I'm suspect. A text message from my poker buddy:
*Your keys are in your purse by the couch.
Text me to say you're still kicking.*
Cat's get nine lives. How many
for drunk bitches who never eat dinner?
I gulp applesauce straight from the jar
to gentle the night's damage. Strip the bed,
pull a sleeping bag over the bare mattress.
On TV "The Walking Dead" are zombies.
I fall over in the shower. I am living
my uncle's death march. When his mistress found him,
his fire liver burned out, a bloodbath for one
retched across his second bankruptcy home,
did she feel relieved? I can sing *hello coffin*
to the full-length mirror and write a grant proposal
for spring. Multitasking is the new norm.
The sun's already quit today. What is a darkness
and what is a black hole? What is a cousin
and what is a pallbearer? Some questions are stupid.
I've got pickles that'll outlast this lease.
I've got a half-dozen presents under someone's tree.

Lament With Rhinestones and Wonder

I carried John in a small sparkle pierced wound
above thin upper lip—*A beauty mark like Marilyn*
he explained, his voice stoned and astral, sweet
lilt so hushed you'd think he was afraid of waking

years of ashes lining the unfinished attic
hotbox. College: good years for fantastic.
Say the glass pipe tasted like diamonds and Paris.
I'll listen. The band below reverberating electric hype

through floor beams—cute little drummer of paradise
got his eyes on my mouth. *Girl*, John said. *Get it
while it's good.* We were good in the night,
the glory stars all ours for following south

toward the wide grid wards of Chicago like so many
misfit Michiganders. Alone in public, I deserted
a gallery dizzy with drunken city believers, lamenting:
What am I doing that keeps leaving me rotten-handed?

The late shift piercer at Tattoo Factory in Uptown
asked if I was sober, if I was sure. One beer all night
but manic as the lake wind, I'd have taken a dozen
fat needles in my face if he and my checking account

would've approved the only beauty I could believe:
something violent and shiny. I'd been putting it to bed
for years with spiked teas and Nyquil, adoring
how it could be heard even without words. Its power

like mirrors: pitiless, everywhere. I wonder
if I'd taken the El downtown, the Jackson 6 south
to Cove Lounge or Bar Louie, if I could've sighted
your wetted silver stud sticky with gin and tonic,

if there could be a story where you and I
met wearing our sad human suits and were saved
somehow by the company, by the not welling
alone with the hell of it. If a wreck like me

could've stopped the newspaper headlines:
the young man, brilliant of course, dangling
from the bound sky of the university geo lab.
In the shrunken obituary photo, the starlet

glimmer pain still there, hair bleached platinum—
I was making myself in this image, John.
My hair already pale straw the day I learned
you were done and put my beasts to rest

in a pill-softened bed. In a queen-less drab town,
the gilt bead flew from the steel hardware's end
under the gust of a full-lunged flu sneeze,
and the two-year-old hole sealed shut too quick

to slide a twenty over a glass counter and ask
to replace the familiar mark. Beware of the mouth:
just half an hour and it starts to heal. John,
I keep waiting for your face to close.

Protest

We are marching in Washington
against the War in Iraq
and you are the bravery
I want to be.
I am following you.
It is 2005 and I am in love
with being next to you.
It is fall. We don't notice
there are no cherry blossoms left.

You don't know,
I never told you, that July
I tried to swallow
all the flies but didn't die.
Only four months later
and I am in love with marching
in Washington, holding
my protest sign,
following after you. John,

It's 2011. I can't stop seeing you
hang from the university.
It's not true.
I wasn't there. I don't know
what clothes you wore,
if your hair was bleached
like the obit pic. I keep saying this
isn't even my death to grieve
and grieve a little more.

Against Ghosts

Come put your dusky coos to rest
in this orchard where the last apples cling
despite, no—to spite, the siren cold wind.
I call the dogs back, gone too far out
into the liminal: Wood lines
disappearing into lowering dark: Oh,
my Ithaca. These two rescues, the pit bull
chasing after the fox hound, bark
for the empty. I am trying fierce this year
to leave my dead alone. Dear _____,
you spit their eyes back animate or quit with it.
        You hear me. I need
        how this space has no echo.

Hush Now

The year I stopped speaking in school
was a year of Laura Ingalls Wilder
and American Girls teaching me
children were better seen
than heard. At recess, once the cold came
to lay its claim on Michigan,
the teacher let me stay in
while the others broached the unkindness
of the icicled playground—
I added up pretend orders from catalogues,
calculating shipping and tax: math,
already a game I could master
but not win. The Felicity doll,
more expensive than two weeks' dinners.
Some nights I'd cradle the possibilities
of her petticoats and corsets:
Belly, that was a thing that was mine
that my father poked and called
chubby. That was the thing
my mother kept growing
like a birthday balloon being puffed
by a big man's lungs until my brother
was born. Something uncertain
spawned in my dreams. Michelle,
the first babysitter, studied botany
and told stories of terrors she wanted
to cure: Ebola, my brain kept deciding
would be the worst end to me.
Each night a woman traversed the ocean
to rub her bloody eyes in my eyes.

Africa was vicious on television,
when it made the bedtime news.
The woman, her hair wrapped
in colorful cloth, wanted to drip her
sickness into me. Lady and Spunky,
the first cats to love me, got Feline Leukemia,
kitty AIDS, the veterinarian said.
Spunky died first. He dragged
his ragged frame into the woods to be alone
with it: winter, the embarrassed
terror of a failing body: *It's natural,*
my mother said, *to seek privacy.*
Michelle's book said AIDS was a disease
that came from needles and blood.

My mother had cushions full of needles
and pins with pearly pink heads.
When there was time for prettiness,
she invented dresses out of floral cloth
and discount Simplicity patterns.
It was not a good year for new church clothes.
Mom had trouble rising from bed
to greet my brother's hungry mouth, the sun
my constant asking and sounding.
I'd learn the words *postpartum depression*
six years later in health class.
Ten years later I'd learn her body wouldn't
stop bleeding. *Tired,* was a word
I knew well: I'd get off the bus ready
to burst with the stories I'd held in
like breath gathered to wish upon candles
or white-headed dandelions. *What do you need,*
some attention? a still voice scolds the air.

Bourbon

after Franz Wright

I can see something a little shaky behind
your left eye. A spooked mule
hauling your mind out of this pleasant
gathering of academics:

One esteemed novelist says,
*Do you have a question
for me? I'm here. I can tell you things.*

And at least he's being honest
about how he sees you as less than
his drunk brain.

I like how your uncertain fingers tap
the wood bar as your credit card barrels
toward maxed out.
Doesn't each ladylike knuckle love me
more than men?

I don't think you're meek. Not
in heels and lipstick.
You just need a little help
brightening.

Let's arch your shoulders
like an angry cat. But not gentle like in yoga.
Hard like the strays that screech in your backyard
tearing blood out of each other.

Can we be dancing now?
Somebody will join
if we're pretty. Aren't we pretty?

Stepping Inside of November

RAZZLE DAZZLE LITTLE PLUGGED-IN SUN!
    I raise my dry face to you O BLUE
LITEBOOK, O HONEYCOMB DAYGLOW—
        don't you know I love you
like aspirin? Like everything invented
to bear what we've been left with: DISGRACE: the hillside
        in its slush clothes could use a little lipstick.
Wouldn't we all feel better if psychiatrists
decorated the sky with golden bows and champagne?
        So I don't really like gold or fizz,
        more of a silver and scotch kind of gal,
but imagine I'm someone who likes the right things:
        cellophane-wrapped candies, ten shades
        of mauve nail polish, kale and commandments.
What's that you say? All of this joy can be had
        for the simple price of
        getting the fuck over myself.
How about I try a little fondness on for a change.
        If I knit a soft blue scarf.
        If I enjoy the tiny loops, effort for warmth and style.
If I call you HELIOS. Then?

Daily Weather

2012
Always too much self
in the morning oatmeal, the news, the weather:
every thing a sign, every sign unbearable.

Another hot toddy autumn, whiskey
poured heavy in a floral teacup
to quell gray doom after gray noon.

Glare at the glisten of early iced oaks:
Beauty, no longer a felt thing
—gutted galleries, artless wind—

Miss a series of calendar entries
in dread clothes: therapy,
office hours, lunch dates, waxing.

The dead are not like anything.
Nobody tastes their mouths.
Don't be like them.

For the holiday party with colleagues
who like nice things
(goat cheese, cabernet, endless kale),

wriggle into nylons that hide
half the season's pale,
a black jersey dress that hangs.

Be a nice thing until midnight.
Then, maybe stomp or sneak off:
the sweaty belly of a club,

unfamiliar forms two-stepping toward
embrace that does not assume love
or even consider it.

Be fire, not this ash
slipping through the long fingers
of a silent god.

My heavens, there are fingers
tugging belt loops toward the living
world of yes and tingle.

Open. Be a good house
for the weary. Say *I do*
to everything that quickens.

In the morning, write: *Flowers! New
red boots! I have no dead in my bed.
My bones are regal. I will stay.*

Never write: *Such a chore, coaxing
survival. I am so tired of it
being my own.*

2013

There's always too much dread in the morning oatmeal, the news, the weather: every thing a sign, every sign a noisy mess. Jesus didn't brush his teeth either. It's just another hot toddy autumn, whiskey poured heavy in a floral teacup to quell the clichéd doom of gray noon. Even elephants have rituals, visit their sundried dead in the field for days weeping big elephant tears, prodding the body with tusk and trunk. Scribble monsters on the hillside until the ground gobbles your firstborn. Miscarriage is common. It's okay if you've bled through the mattress pad. Call it a miracle. No child stealing calcium from your bones. Thank God. Call in to work *eccentric*. No, *pink eye*. No, something unrelated to excrement. Don't say: *I didn't even know I was pregnant*. Maybe you weren't. Just a clotted mass of failure trying to get out. All ghost names are lies. Maybe this isn't your story. Who says it's mine? I'm a nun or infertile, an infertile nun, never went home with a man from a bar because he was wearing chainmail, never was bored or thirsty or the kind of alone that needs a witness. I'm the kind of gal God sends peonies by the dozen, a vase for every windowsill and end table. How thoughtful. I try to imagine how wise hands that arranged clouds out of atoms and wild magic must be. It's true, the landscape listens. I'll say something loving for a change: *I've tasted the sky in a book and am writing its sequel: lavender, lavender, lavender.*

2014

There's always too much America in the morning
oatmeal, the news, the weather:
every thing a sign, every sign sanguine.
I glare at the glisten of early iced oaks
for insisting upon beauty.
It's another hot toddy autumn,
whiskey poured heavy in my floral teacup
to hush the vain doom of gray noon.
I haven't talked to the sky in years,
haven't said bless the soft skin
behind the knees of every man and woman
I've loved. Haven't said please.
Let heaven be thick with honey and lemon,
a warm dream of *yes* and *plenty*.
Let heaven be. I need to believe
beyond this unevenly patrolled ground
the hunted jump up from chalked outlines.
Even elephants have mourning rituals,
visit their sundried dead in the field for days
weeping big elephant tears, prodding
the body with tusk and trunk.
The cops who left Michael Brown dead
in the street for four hours—what were they?
Someone call Ghostbusters or the UN.
I don't want to mother in this country.
Let all my 60,000 remaining eggs
become woundless and un-wounding blood.

Humanly

I asked you to speak back. Instead,
all these damn starlings. Who am I
kidding? I don't know shit about birds.
I know whatever kind they are, they have come
and you have not. I know absence,
an old lover, is the opposite of kindness.
If I string the night between two fence posts,
one side heaven and one side hell,
if I stand in the middle of the field
with a bottle of wine, human
and raging, my friends will still hang
from the line like the earth's dirty laundry,
my feet just sinking in the mud
that is not a grave, not tonight.

Take

We Were Trying to Write a Love Story

But were we flailing
on the bare, rough mattress or failing?
If to fail is to want wilderness and to achieve
only small puddles of salt—
if to salt is what we do to wounds
to make them feel more wound-like,
then we must've been filling
our anatomies with stinging,
which was a failure at mercy,
which is a component of loving I'm told.

Did I hear him singing
a blues that bent August into a room
with no windows to cool the viscous
night? It must be possible
to bust a woman open like a window
in a cinema chase scene: that shatter sound,
the wrecking hilt behind his blues.
He must have tried to jump
through me. He must have tired
his jumping muscles.

Could I ever have borne him
into the glad light of spring?
Do I mean borne or raised and can love
raise a sad-boned man into anything
like light? If to find blood
strung through the thick yellow of
a store-bought egg is to bear sadness,

if we were scared to eat it
and threw it away,
then aren't we just dumb
humans: sweat-soaked, sweet-
seeking, and in some books saved?

This is just to say...

I have taken
the tongue of the man you love
—which you were probably wanting
six state lines away—
between my glad thighs,
and thought not of
the damped wool clothing
his chin, not
the baritone begging
for a long drink,
not the human-shaped stain
haunting the ceiling,
but of you
as I came—your face
slammed shut
at the sight of him
delighting in the trembling
current eddying
me. Do not forget
the moan I left
in his scrumptious ears:
it was meant for you.

The Diplomat

His body, a throne
            I bow down to—

He knows this: power
begins with knowing

you can beget the loaves
and the fishes from

your leftovers, that each miracle
is yours. He rips

the delicate lace of a silk slip
            that once curtained

my mother's slim hips, that
I've hand-washed

in four apartments, two
            countries, three cities

with a level of care akin
to worship. It's true

I let some animal desiccate
            in the skillet and never

prayed for it. I deserve this
            staggered violence of

teeth digging into the soft
        pale fruit of my neck.

In the morning I will admire
        my starched and ironed lapel,

blazer tapered at the waist,
        infinity scarf draped

around purpled collarbone,
        the unworried line

of his brow, the altar
        I've made in this image.

The Beast

The shaved prickly skin
of his boxer chest won't stop
graphing itself onto me,
an ugly night garment
I wake in. I still have legs
and organs, everything
I need to leave him
with his dumb mouth
shocked open. I could
reach toward the slim neck
of a bottle or a slighter
man and not be sorry.
The world would have to
forgive my imprudence.
I could sneak my garbage
body into a gleaned man's bed
like women's magazines say
I should, leave traces
of my glamour, amulets,
lingerie in bed sheets.
Tell me there's a body
that isn't his, that can solve
the way I want the whirring
nonstop of cars to come
just a little closer to
smashing the room in.

Blurred Lines

"But you're an animal, baby, it's in your nature.
Just let me liberate you"

—*Robin Thicke*

We, the predators, lost and hungry,
we, the big teeth, the hard shoulders,
we, the body, we the spirit of fast,

are licking the salt off necks again,
answering the questions
of splayed shaved bodies with questions:

Can you live without pleasure?
Doesn't it feel good
to be eaten from the cunt
to the heart?

When the bitch sun lies down,
when we are left with absence
in bars asking heat from rum
and rum-filled bodies,
we can find no gods
beyond the beast of speed.

It's gotten us this far,
never left us alone
in a crowded department store
with nervous genitals and tears,
better than our mothers.

We know all the nasty things about you:
How you watch the pantry moths
writhe in glue traps. How you
were born with thirst from head
to curled toes, Girl.

Manners

We lady beasts got mouthfuls of daisies.
We lady beasts got stems stuck in teeth.
Our sweet-seeking tongue tips, they catch
and canker out of obsession into tender.
You little playground beast, I could
render you toothless, mouth dull
as your gaze, pluck your mane bald,
butcher your face, rend you
as mangy outside as in, little beast.
I could but will not devour you.
Now where are my flowers?
What blood force raised you?
We lady beasts got lace up our asses,
got wax burns, suck in and in
until we look like good lady beasts
blue-faced and beaming.
Where did you go with those ears
I could nibble into nothings,
loving the cartilage chew in my teeth,
tough as desire is. It took hours
to prepare my face for this dinner
with you slobber-grinned,
slurping slop from the waitress's waist.
I've come to steep broth from your bones.

Sugar & Spice

I would I were as sweet as honey, Bunny.
Catch more flies—I know but
who wants flies? Such harbingers of death,
just ask Dickinson.

If I sprinkle a little Splenda in this blood,
if I bake a banana cream pie and don't cry,
throw all the citrus in a garbage bin,
coat the apartment in Miraculin,
might your teeth rot rank with joy?

And you'll be the toothless fool grinning,
and I the fairy sugar wife,
and we'll grow globular together,
hold the couch cushions down with force—
if only I were anything nice.

Come Ye Faithful Savior Man

Welcome to the coliseum of my body,
the last shit-show before the dreck
innards of Lake Erie summon you
into their drown and doubt,
dread sirens. I have housed death-
matches in my gullet: five times
the will of each organ
to subsist has trumped the will
of the mouthy *I* to not—
to plunge into the flickering
dark of noxious drams, deluged
liver interring the room.
Watch me. I swallow swords
for diversion. Come marvel
at my distended esophagus stretched
too far, too many times
around the whetted dare.
I house multitudes of predators,
lions and tigers and bears sharpening
their fangs for you. Oh, my
dim-hearted darling, we will have to
dine on your patchy chest hair
and nonchalance. Applaud
my lip-licking gnash as I prepare
to devour you in nibbles of rib
meat and man feet, please. Sugar-dick,
Cum-dumpling, weren't you bored
limp holding manicured hands at matinees?
I've got your ticket stashed in a jar
of teeth or pills, pills with teeth. Ready.

For a Daughter Never to Be Born

First there is a sky I like and then there is the same sky
grayed and without wanting:
I want to give you something better, a castle
in the sky-blue-crayon heavens where the fridges are filled
with chocolate that's the perfect degree of sweet
and it's all our bodies need.

I fold my hands under the table and pick at hangnails
until they bleed spidery red shapes on the napkin
while a man-child who wants to hold your head in his hands
talks endlessly of futures
where I am someone who's happy
to eat shrimp scampi and watch a John Hughes flick
and call it a good life.

I have my grandmother's elegant hands,
long nail-beds, fingers so thin all rings require resizing:
there is something good in me
that I won't be giving you.

Genesis of the Only Michigander
Who Doesn't Drive

Mom's in the passenger seat of the family minivan, fear-
braced against the door each time
I stop or turn or accelerate, yammering about my cousin
again: *Such a little hussie.*
And her parents, my aunt and uncle, *uninvolved, clueless.*
A four-way intersection,
early evening traffic stretching, a red light
speaking its cautions. *How many abortions,*
how many adoptions does it take? Someone ought to
just spay her like a dog!
So much depends upon wanting the right things:
to be alive next to
an alive body; the car not on fire, not splayed open
showing its violent machinery.
Mom's mouth is full of wicked names for girls
like me. My body, full-shame—
full-fury I can end as easily as not.
I count the cocks I've been touched by
and thank each blood-filled one
for never planting anything noticeable in me.
I've never been good at wanting the right things.

Lost Prayer From Adolescence

First car I see tonight I wish I may
I wish might crawl through the shotgun window
and go wherever the going go.

For years there were no mirrors
in our quiet home. My mother finds
her mother's ghost in my eyes

strangers call pretty—their big doe
wonder, a cancer that won't let go.
I am always the reason the house breaks

into bills. Even when I'm gone,
I am the curse that throws tomatoes
against the walls, cuts the screen,

kicks the dog. Guilty until proven
alibied—I know there is something shameful
about being alive in this hunted body

with its reminders, with its questions.

Christmas in Chicago

My suitcase barely dropped off
in my sweetest friend's living room,
and I'm making excuses to leave:
an errand, I've forgotten impossible things,
eyeliner, pantyhose, antihistamines
to guard against Apple Juice (the cat).
I don't say that the law student left me
with so much pain I thought *kidney stones*
until the rot came—that I stared
at my soiled panties in the plane lavatory
until a flight attendant knocked.
I take the Brown Line to Belmont
and transfer to Red, stare out the platform
at Boystown, frozen quiet, too early
to be dizzied with dancing and pleather.
I always thought I'd rage if a man
did this to me, slit his wrists or mine,
but instead I board the second train
and nibble dry cuticles, a tiny raggedness.
At Howard Brown I wait with strangers
for an hour reading the same page of Oppen
to be told the new name for my womb.

Overrun

The never-ending itch comes worst at night,
warm blankets quickening
mites in my skin, trespassers demanding,
*What'd you think you'd find
in his jeans? A receipt?*
I didn't know ruining
would begin in a brief meeting of flesh
and never say when.
I didn't know I'd break and break
until petechiae, until everything went raw
red raving for scalding water,
rubber gloves, another bottle of bleach
and tube of permethrin,
another bottle of wine and wine and wine,
another doctor saying *soon*, or *cure*,
or *it should be over by now*; and it should.

Empress of Solitaire

There once was a man who loved the idea of a woman
like a shiny invention he'd jimmied out of wanting.

There once was a woman who wanted nothing
but to be curtains hanging in an empty room.

There once was a woman who was a room
full of whatchamacallits the man kept taking.

There once was a taking so big the woman
was left with nothing but blood and crumbs.

*

If I shave off the hair strands he touched,
will my nicked scalp,
the skull's shape I've never seen,
be my own to love or hate?

If I hack off the hand being tugged
through space and time,
a little sanguine Valentine, then
will the pain and ridiculous scabbed stump
please be mine? Be only mine.

*

I am kidnapping myself, leaving no gumdrop trail.

This chipped black nail polish, coffee grounds on

the kitchen floor, unchanged hall light bulb, medium

boobs, large tattoos, small shoes, zits, sunburn, loud

lonely, slurred dancing, bad credit—

Boundaries

I drew my *no* line early
that first night on tour in his city,
what I wanted   what I didn't.

In the whiskey morning my naked trapped
on the wrong side.
Too broke for a hotel, I stayed.

When he pulled my panties down,
said, *You asked what was special
about Arkansas,* I told myself
it would be easier if I just said yes.

Nothing easy about giving up
your body like a white flag for five months.

I moved my office to bed
and grew wide enough to lie down in.
The rubbing of thighs became a sign:
might as well just stay. Little gut,
an anvil pinning me down.

Every deck was stacked with old maid cards.
Such a nice guy, all my friends said,
all my friends say.

Last Dinner

Not the whole bogus heart but the slice of it
you said was carved out just for me,
I am eating grilled over a bed of arugula—
Chicken, the waiter says. And you stare down
at the drizzled balsamic on my plate,
then at your own tender cut of meat, and nod.
Hunger, a gnashing thing, has always struck you
as too vulgar a habit for a toothsome lady.
I can see your disgust as I pick the greens
from betwixt incisors with an unadorned nail.
A tethered urgency funnels white wine
down your throat: *Oh God stay still still*,
my mind soothsays—the function of drink,
an uncertain anchor we both lower in faith.

Post-Theist Logic

I march against sexual
violence & a man I know
best as a brunch-maker
& worst as the slippery
agreement between whiskey
& *yes*, is holding a sign
that says, *consent is
sexy.* I remember the flame,
the hole his cigarette left
on my silver blouse,
& know it's not the same
as the burn victim I saw
on the subway—I was ashamed
to see everyone's terror at her
aliened face, her quiet
suggestion of what can be
endured. In my monster life,
a cold man on the bus needs
heat, & I give it to him.
Fear rides him as he watches
each limb learn to glow,
then ash. I give him my hand
& say, *This scar is yours*—
which is half of why I am
alone. I'm told freedom is
a credit limit increase
& an apartment of one's own.
I can buy every glimmer
I want, except God,

which is the other half
of why. I still pray
with these clammy hands.

Twirling the Darkness in a Holiday Inn

I cannot recall what hue or pattern
the comforter bore but it had been discarded
to the floor nearly a decade ago—I was
watching myself in the hotel mirror to make sure
my body was still happening despite
the flesh-knife gutting me.
Deep in the blue trouble of my young
consent, I knew there were two kinds of men, then:

    The ones playing hold 'em—these
    four thronged round the table
    two body-lengths away from
    the footboard, cursing losses
    into beer-drenched hands.
    Their musty absence of caring
    I have learned to call night—
    lightless garments gagging
    my unheeded gasp.

    The one above me, nothing
    like God, he said he made me
    woman out of his coming. Again
    and again, he spells his name
    in an archive of hotel sheets.
    And he says, *Let there be*
    taking. And there is
    blood that wants to escape
    the frame that I animate.

But we, my almost love, we are above
the ivory linens, and there is nothing merciless
in your hand giving itself to my moan,
wanted more exuberantly than sleep.
Or rather, I am a mobile twirling
the darkness, an ornament keeping vigil
over unalarmed flesh. I monitor
the room as it lacerates my past
self with violent indifference toward theft
and the imprecise edges that fence
the void, the wound, the whatever is
left to do the weeping after
you wake birdless, noose-skied.

In the morning I will worry I'm the wrinkle
wriggling across your placid skin,
a little parasitic in my need for company—
a conquering dance slithering beneath
the contract of each embrace.
I will press you into a book, into ink
smears and fading. And it's true
you said yes to tapas in Alphabet City,
to the last neck-craning seats in a theatre
where poets tried out laughter on stage,
to the bartender's chaotic wink,
to this bed that yawns with lamplight.
It's true we split the bill to nestle
into this temporary bargain comfort.

Revisionist History

I need a new story. I want a daughter:

Let it be said that the girl in the prey pose
knew so much of her beauty
she roared the baseball player's ears deaf
before biting the right one off Mike Tyson style.

Let it be said that upon losing music
the man wept himself into
a drowned boy—
and the girl, seeing his ache
was its own ocean, dredged
his limp behind back to shore.

Let it be said that when the man rose
unchanged by mercy,
the girl's incisors were filed sharp as shanks
as her mother had told her best suited ladies
in the wilds of home team nights.

Let it be said that her mother
was a butcher. That she knew how
to gut a mammal without waste.

That she never looked back.

Fang and Fantasy

To Mania

Which witch this scuttling is: I am and have been

       what goes *drown* in the night, what lost fathoms spit back

dripping magic, some of it good, most of it obscene.

       I think I've known your house within the winter snow

too well. I've knelt there with iced knees and tremble,

       tapped —*Luck, luck, noose. Luck, fuck, noose*—chased

your gilt blood drama ending, your damsel terror tarantella,

       round and round the bound sky of my ordinary skull.

I'd like you to redecorate me. Dance me blue hair dizzy.

       Fuck me sideways with that gaudy tambourine.

It's a party. I'll buy the flowers. Drink the wine myself.

Pretty Death Myths

I. Gorge

I've spent months peering up your neglected
undercarriage, the wind inflating your skirt
so I can see the tired lingerie you wear,
reasoning: *Who is left to care*
about a little worn lace?
My loveliness is deathless.
My mouth is grander than any mouth
you've ever stumbled into,
more capable of answering want: Darling,
my middle name is *Yes*.
At the edge of my greenery there is a cool,
clear pool that is ready to cleanse
your witching hour sweats.
I know you see bad skies
on your eyelids. I know you
are tired of seeking
shelter. I can give back
the unclenched jaw of childhood,
the torched wooden jungle gym,
every pillaged inch. I have been fenced in
by men with limited capacities
for splendor. Do not let them deny you
entry to the grace of my gravity.

II. *Steering Wheel*

Isn't the guardrail looking quite dapper tonight
in his silver and starshine?
I could take you there, beyond
sturdy steel to the woods that hum a wedding march:
Elsa's Procession to the Cathedral, your favorite
Wagner, remember: You were once a wind
piercing the belly of an orchestra,
a studied clarinetist, loving best to play
for the accepting silence of floral wallpaper.
Remember the brown liquor it took to not shake
through rehearsals. The missed solos,
the conductor's baffled glare saying,
But you have nothing to be nervous about.
Don't you want to be held by that song,
the trees, your limbs breaking against theirs
in an endless marriage. Isn't that love?

III. *Barbiturates*

Call on me—Follow me—If you swallow me, I'll swallow you—.

Throng Hour

"I myself am hell;
nobody's here"

—*Robert Lowell*

If I fail nine kinds of kindness in the year of chalk-dry luck
If I walk into the hulked throat ruin

If the lights turn drown
If I hermit and eye sore moonlight
If I am the lone skunk in my churchyard
If I stand on top of my skull and look in at the sour swill
If my mind's not right
If I take an awl to the hide that keeps me
If I am a grave fairy of ill-spirit from hull to hull
If I scare and bear the town in fishnets
If I peer into fall's gorge and feel bloodless,

What I can say for myself is this:
I won't leave a dead body in the kitchen
for my darlings to find.

I won't have darlings.

Effort at Music With Bloody Hands

The morning after the night boxing walls,
swollen fingers stiff with old blood
gingerly, with grimace, pluck out
"Ode to Joy," the first tune I taught them:
As long as I'm living they'll have this song.

Even in this room of broken glass,
all my anger compounded for a split second
into the wrist snap, the follow through
I spent years trying to get right in softball,
to get all the power my arms could give,

I've got it. Good thing I'm weak, I think
examining the undented wall, small blood
smear where knuckles opened, nothing
unwashable. At least the animal hauling
my mind around town is a live one.

Epiphany or Die

My hand grasped the knife
easy like chopping carrots and onions
on a Saturday when there's no rush to dine,
as I crushed a Lamictal gorge
into numb heaven snow
on the wooden cutting board
an ex had sent in a gift basket
with sharp cheddar and cabernet
the day before I left him for quiet,
to be alone with my alone.
After chasing the powder with tap water,
I put the dishes in the sink,
as if I would rinse them the next morning,
load and run the dishwasher
like a good roommate.
When I tucked into endless bed,
I pulled the comforter, a graphic green print
I'd bought to cheer me through winter,
up to my nose, stretched my limbs
to the full edges, and said *wait*.
When I tiptoed to the bathroom,
took a pink toothbrush to my throat
to purge what I could,
I felt a clammy suctioning,
an old cold song clamping down.
I tried calmly to stand,
to get my phone and call an ambulance,
but my legs were already not mine:
forehead rolling tile, puked bathmat,

walls floor stand floor walls fall.
I had one choice, to scream
or die. E, M, I'm sorry
I woke you. I wanted to live.

In the Psych Ward

A choking terror detonates the psych ward:
drug-blank faces of fellow patients who mind
their minds, who converse with shadows, won't eat
or bathe until sweethearts call and beg they try
at being, at swallowing swill and saying please,
ask what must be kept down to leave, get told nothing.

Friends come, ask what I need, I say nothing;
I am nothing but furniture to this ward.
Guilty as a white jailbird, I am the worst warden to please:
How could you? How could I? Why mind
autumn for the sum of its deaths and not try
at fixing something simple, something salty to eat.

Stomach scoured raw with pill dust, I eat
fruit cocktail, limp veggies, want nothing
but am told I can't get out if I don't try
to be the tasty fairy of cheer sugaring the ward,
chin up, giving up the gray ghosts of my mind
that say, *Damselcunt, Call our names sweet, please.*

Here, Doctor, my chapped little hooves, if you please,
take their measly bites of meat. I am no good to eat
but will pay a thousand bucks a day for you to chew my mind
into something that purrs gently, stirs for nothing.
I give you my word—(*disorder*)—I'll shine up this ward
with whatever chemicals you'll give me. I'll try to try.

Herr Doktor, I'm tired of speaking of how I tried
to get out of this body. How I failed. Please,
can I have a pen again? Dark words aren't wards.
Nothing but sporks to cut gristle, we use fingers to eat.
Someone's carved, *Help! I'm Alive*, into ecru with nothing,
someone with ingenuity, a razor spangled mind.

Dread in the heart, heart in the fatty mind,
I pretzel my legs, breathe, give meditation a try,
mutter my mantra quietly: *Let me be nothing,*
Let me be not a thing, Let me be. Please?
I'll eat all the sour milk shit I'm given to eat.
I'll not touch all the mirrors. I'll take life as my ward.

O mind of thunder, mind of thick night, please
the white coats, try, say the drugs work, eat,
censure nothing-wishes with vigilant ward.

Menstruation at Twenty-Six

after Anne Sexton

This myth I can't get over: the punishment
of dead leaves, cold pastorals.
I glut and glut the jeweled seeds,
stomach filled more by the next world than life.
Dreaming up a daughter sobbing
in christening frills, the uncertain
life I could give of this constant autumnal
body I've fed death and wept as it spat
those gray eyes back out like rotten greens,
I praise the thick ruby oozing of the never
conceived, the latex-guarded nothings.
I am afraid of the moving mouths
of doctors, what they'll say has been done
to my liver and bowels by wee fistfuls
of quieting pills. With bruised inner elbows
of iv saviors, gimped life of a body
even paramedics wouldn't hold,
dropped down the staircase like a limp fish,
I am my monster. Must be a sin in it,
to wish a child born to a half-poisoned mother.
I'd pilfer joy from first curls and coos,
damn the dimpled dear into dread clothes
and rioting the common ebb of seasons.
We all know what a dirge sounds like.
No need for another pitchy voice droning:
poor old me, burry me, marry me
to worms, let the pallbearers carry me.

What Was the Most Delicate Thing
in the Psych Ward?
after Roger Reeves

Paula, terrified of being sent back to Binghamton,
the closest long-term facility
where you never know who's
gonna try to kill you,
played board games, usually Parcheesi,
with a man I assumed to be her husband
or brother, who came each day
during visiting hours after lunch.
When a nurse said I wasn't
a lifer, wouldn't need to spend
my days in and out of hospitals,
I wept, trying to imagine who
would have come to sit with me
if my life wasn't mine to decide,
if I couldn't get myself back from
that side: Lenny in hospital scrubs
all week, nobody would bring him
his clothes, howled Bob Marley
outside my room. After the third day,
people stopped coming to visit;
at least someone brought my glasses,
slippers, underwear, sweatpants
without a drawstring
so I couldn't hang myself.

Dear Critic,

You can chant *bitch, weak thing, idiot,*
all night if you want.
Tell me all the slutty things about my hands,
how they didn't fight the bearded man off
when he dragged me back into the apartment
after I'd started to run,
how I'll always smell like him, menthol
shaving cream deposited deep in my dermis.
Tell me I'll never get over it, running
out of apartments, out of towns,
out of my body again and again
the paramedics siphoning me back in,
fluids, charcoal, whatever it takes
to make a woman live. Tell me
I don't deserve it, this life, this cozy body
no man has touched since August,
this bed, lavender sheets, clean
as I want them. You can call me
all my nastiest names. I am shutting
myself into my quietest room,
barricading all the roads with heavy furniture.
You'll have to find a new girl to ruin.

Thanksgiving Poem

It's the night before Thanksgiving
and a woman I love leaves a small feast
bagged and paid for in the cart and drives off
because a woman she loves has lost
a child to a decade of cancer.
I don't want to tell her
about the overdose last month,
as if my survival were subsidized
by arbitrary deaths. Ground,
why gobble hearts that are wanted
in graduation gowns and laurels
but leave this deadbeat that runs me
keeping its sloppy time? Soft Cradle,
Star Ladle in the sky so high,
teach me to bless the lavender and blood
things this boy's body won't become,
to hold my knees to my chest
and say, *Yes, I have all these things*
I can still touch with my hands.

I Keep Trying to Functional

But then I run into my ex-AA sponsor at a lake house party
that my new café boss is throwing,
and I'm holding a local IPA, Flower Power,
and I'm not drunk, not like I used to get, but still
I could disappear into her questioning nod—
the what if I fall back into obliterate skull,
into fuck the puffy scar of sixteen in an airport motel
when I didn't say no exactly;
I'd given up on that. Already,
I am teetering before the bonfire, doing nothing
wrong per se, letting the smoke chase me
in a circle around the pit.

Take as Needed

The angels of Klonopin put me back in my body
for the afternoon. How easy
it could be to up the dosage until I am all kind and dumb,
pleading nothing to the gods who do nothing.
How many milligrams does it take to get to the center
of the mind's tornado, that calm eye?
How many more to stay there
while the café orders come in,
fingers stabbing gently at the register,
a boss eyeing a survival poem tattooed
on my forearm, *Do you have another job*
as a billboard? I smile as hard as I can.
It can be easy to feed people
who aren't myself. To carry plates with omelets
and smile at old ladies who order decaf,
which means making a fresh French press,
which is effort but easy as pills.
There is a quiet I can't explain where
there used to be fast music shaking the room.

A Little Effort, I'm Told, Is All I Need

Everywhere mountains. I can't move the light switch.

Did you know the sky is closed to mourners?

My hands, the closest I've got to a gravestone.

I've been picking small flowers at nail beds.

The suicide, a boulder I roll away from my body's cave.

Each day I begin with song / the opposite of poison:

this mouth has tasted such warm stews.

To Do:

Put three days' musty clothes from the floor into the only
empty laundry basket. Call this progress. The landlord's
coming to fix the toilet in the morning. Somebody raised
you. That's a lie. It's a week's clothes. Clean eyeliner shav-
ings and toothpaste from the sink. See above.

Draft a poem about the impending breakup the entire
city of Boston will hold against you until death. No, draft
a poem where you are forgiven. There's such a need for
fantasy. Try on your mother's wedding dress. No, it's 6
sizes too small. No, she gave it away. She wanted it gone.
You're not even near her. You left. You were never given.
This is your one power.

Buy ice cream. Ben & Jerry's. Go all out like it's payday.
The loan companies will call regardless of this $3.95. It's
not that you've earned it, but you haven't not earned it.
Isn't that America?

Drink a glass of wine. You bought Malbec. The storeowner
said it was the quintessential Malbec. The precise thing he
thought customers wanted when they said *Malbec*. That
it was *jammy*. It was $12 and called PILKE, which made
you think of Rilke, who makes you want to change your
life, which makes you need wine.

Remember your toilet won't stop running. Shut the water
off after the tank's filled up. Don't drink so much that you
forget about the toilet not working right. Don't drink so

much that you're in bed hungover when the landlord comes to fix things in the morning. A new valve he said and showed you a black part that must have been a valve. Act like somebody raised you.

After the Psych Ward

I'm trying to be precise. When I say
the sky got so heavy I couldn't walk,
I mean I crumbled up in bed every weekend
for two months eating nothing
but delivery, Massaman curry
or sausage pizza. Having given up
on gossip, my pariah dance
the story the department kept telling,
I spoke only to teach, taught only
to keep my health insurance,
to not add *financial*
to my list of ruins. I wrote no poems.
Nothing would speak to me—
my brain a fogged balloon,
only had two words: pop or shrink.

Witch and Dirty Wardrobe

after Jamaica Kincaid

This is how water can be fire. This is how to shower five

times a day. This how to wait for the next boot to fall. This

is how to burn a red moon into your thigh with coffee

and stain linen trousers. This is how to drop a file in the

hallway and scoop up the papers, disordered. Disordered:

this is how to keep on living. To keep on living, you will

need to drown the misfiring brain with white wine until

it flatlines. The "down to earth drug" they call it, which

is to say groggy but unconcerned by the temporality of

bloomed crocuses. This is how to be dragged out of bed by

deadlines. This is how to order takeout instead of buying

groceries. This is how to take the bus and turn up head-

phones in silent indifference toward frat boys and children.

This is how to walk to the gorge and praise its myth of

permanence. This is how to delete phone numbers of dead

friends from your contacts list. This is how to keep on

living: dare to scale a cod, to salt its flesh, to eat it alone,

to know there is something good and wanted propelling

your body toward something unknowable.

Why the World Had to End

An editor asks after revisions, the poems about sex, death, limits.
Nothing will speak to me. All the mouths taped shut—
my bed, not holy or ruined, just there, fulfilling its duty.

I am here, my body pulsing and puffing, taking
normal amounts of space and oxygen
in living rooms and offices, my hair dyed new red

and dried to a buoyant shine.

There must be some meaning in staying alive,
but it won't announce itself
in the pharmacy checkout line,
in coffee sips on the bus ride to work,
all this waiting.

    The women came to the courts with garbage in hand, chanting
    I once had such bright fruits. Juice ran down the jurors' chins.

I plunged my rot into a snow bath,
Lamictal crushed on a kitchen cutting board,
choosing to be nothing over what was left.

Here's a revision: I gutted a man with a pool cue
while his pants were down. Don't ask me how.
You know why.

Waiting at the Temp Agency

The grace today is that employers can't see it, the suicide,
unless they look in my eyes hard enough. They can't see
the healed nerve damage that limped me down academic
halls for months, my right foot a dead fish. *Did you fall?*
the hospital nurses kept asking. All I could think was
stairs / paramedics / trying to stand up when I wasn't
anywhere near my body / my poor roommate hauling
me. *Yes*, I'd say, uncertain. *I must have fallen.*

Truce

Bless the manic brain. The *If I have to walk all night*
out of this dank little city I will so help me
brain. The *Do you remember the underwear you wore*
the last night you were raped brain.
The dress, lilac, flowered, the first days of summer.
How you tried to run toward highway,
how he barricaded the door with furniture.
No, you don't remember—
he told you all that with a grin the next day.
Bless the brain at 2 AM asking questions
about funerals, your uncle's ruined liver,
the question mark in your own,
whatever it is that makes the body slow tremor.
Bless the brain that plots its own murder
and writes love poems. Bless the brain that notices
crocuses, remembers birthdays, cookie recipes,
the exact gaze of a lover across a cafe table.
Bless the brain that says yes and no.

Naming What Is Lost, What Remains

after Lynda Hull

Six months my science experiment brain, jimmied quiet
by five drugs a day, has made brief cameos
at downtown bars, joked about burial
in freshman essays. It was pills that nearly took me,
crushed and wanted, witching my blood.
This nodding body, acquiescent,
has an alarm waiting to cockadoodle
deep behind the heavy velvet drapes of Klonopin,
Lamictal, Lexapro, Abilify, Propranolol—
dizzied machinery, dumb and needy,
this little hit-me-harder spirit will wrestle me again,
wake me in panic heart, dream me sweating
in a sunless room. Tonight, spring
is hiding its magic, late April air trembling me.
And it is good to tremble. It is good to kiss April,
to get its rainy taste all over my mouth.

Anchor

Fabulousness

*"The phenomenon [nuclear war] is fabulously textual also to
the extent that, for the moment, a nuclear war has not taken
place: one can only talk and write about it."*

—Jacques Derrida

Danced out and sweaty, with club-stamped hands
and whiskey-wobbled ankles, we four women
direct the cab to The Jackhammer, a 4 AM leather bar
where we can take our tops off and be in love
with our flesh that keeps being good to us,
keeps covering our guts and bones, keeps
glistening beneath bar lights. *Shirts off
or leather,* the bouncer says. I consider my boots,
my motorcycle jacket, the animals
I am wearing—but the point is
to be fabulously bold in our vices for a night.
We huddle shyly like a small herd of caribou,
a full spectrum of breast sizes
in a room full of men with assless chaps
and furry chests. A man says, *It's fabulous
to see women down here;* he says our breasts
are *fabulous* and motorboats Mariah's,
which are the most voluptuous and tempting
in their otherness. In another bar,
I might have slapped him. Here,
in this gaudy light, I want
to kiss his forehead and say
bless you. Here, the prevalence
of pain is made public. Men line up
to be tied to a wooden apparatus,
limbs splayed open and secured

to prevent flailing when the whip
slices their backs. Here, we call pain
pleasurable, as if an apocalypse
can be sequined with joy—
as if it's okay to marvel at the beautiful
cloud of the atom bomb in photos,
at a hell we cannot know until
it owns us. I wonder
what could be made of my skin
by a disease that lurks in both loved
and unloved bodies: human disaster.
There is something ugly in this
worry, in having it here, some remnants
of GRID and Ronald Reagan. Here is a prayer
in praise of the groaning in the backroom:
Let each body be loved until its end.

Long Distance Aubade

Spun in the sugar plum daze of daybreak, your face
across a diner table eating hash browns off my plate
is so here I could wink at it,
could touch my chin signaling to wipe beard crumbs,
could touch your chin signaling
to kiss soon as the waitress isn't looking,
which might be often, the coffee only lukewarm.
Sometimes it's a long time. It's okay. It's a dream.
We tip as much as we can. Most times
I wake alone and gaze at the same sky you gaze at
through broken blinds. I'm certain
it's what you're doing right now as I fumble
for glasses, pick out wrinkled clothes
from a laundry basket, never folded but clean,
brace myself against the too cold
of a stingy landlord who stifles the heat at sixty-three.
I'd rather press my nose into your chest
than teach *Frankenstein* to freshmen.
This is what I do: I wake in a nest of your hair,
which isn't here but smells of peppermint,
kiss where I'd like your brow to be,
leave the bed unmade, wait for the bus
in a puffy down coat. Sometimes it's a long time.
It's okay. There are dreams. We hold
each other as much as we can.

A Blessing

We have come to the Chanticleer to graze
        among the graceless stutter
of neon-washed electronica, spastic metronome
        of collegiate hips. I still harbor
the Pac-Man remains of a peach-pecan pie.
        I have been thorough in my loving:
Real butter for the crust. I sampled a sliver
        from each skinned globe
and only baked the best. We scoop
        the mess out with our hands and lick
our palms clean. Each lifeline says
        keep going. Our thick heels pestle
a paste of stray flakes and beer that sticks
        bodies together like they've never knotted
the cheap veil of morning around a bedpost
        and scurried home. Remember:
each slice is as good as the first. This is a mercy
        we've earned: our mouths, our own.

A Lusting

I know your thighs are giddy
with the promise of clenching—
of a light not unlike the grace flicker
of daybreak during the bleak
of north country winter.
I have made you in this image:
your one leg more pliable
than the other, both saluting
the headboard, the west wall,
his sinew and harbor.
I have been making women
crow and buck since before
the dawning of sin gave me
a bad name, gave you shame.
You can live without tasting
his bountiful nape,
but why would you want to
yield to bland fates
when I have made him salty?

Offering

This is what I have to give you. Leftovers
that aren't vegan, not even food really—
burnt leather scraps for a heart, but my God,
I've been saving them for you.
I'll leave what I have at your feet
like a proud cat littering mice across the stoop.
So this is love. So this is entropy. I'll break
every bone in my feet running toward
the shiny gate of it.
The whole damn sky holds its breath.
Let me be holy and warm.
Let me be the exhale. The best wine.
The wish on every eyelash.

Not Now

My hair was red when I was born
and wants to be again.
The henna grit is trying
to heal what I've been doing to myself
with chemicals—Bleach
is the beginning of the killing
I have believed in
and called *beauty*.
How am I supposed to get all this earth
out of my scalp?

Over a Mexican omelet that said
it was the best in America
but was not the best
for him, my lover spoke French
too beautifully for my hangover,
which is its own perforated ruin.
I want to know more precisely
what he was saying about my face,
the waterfront, the coffee.
Did he find us fair
enough to reach for
once more. I never know
the right language for love
in the early afternoon
when I feel more vessel than art.

Every map means conquest.
There's a scar on my back that holds
the crux of Lake Michigan.
I have been there, in
Chicago. The water couldn't
lull the want.
So many wet their lips
and call the wrong names.
I'd like my father to appear
in the kitchen making French toast,
making stale bread remember
its goodness.

Too exhausted for shame,
I rub my forehead against the doorframe.
Where are my eyes for weeping with?
The test is negative,
which is good, unless you want
it. I could want to make life
out of foolishness.
Sometimes I am too much. Love,
come: Eat all of my strawberries.
It is summer and they are ready.
I will not need them
for this belly that stretches
around nothing.

Good Vision

Having already taken my eyes out
for the night, I cannot discern
what my lover's face is doing
in the dim lamp light—mood lighting,
it's called by those who can see
to see the defects of another's body,
of their own.

Each year, the optometrist says
my capacity for unaided wonder
in cheekbones and hillsides
has lessened, is lessening,
is moving toward nostalgia.

Memory: It is Sunday. I am nine,
rousing my mother from bed
with coffee. Her eyes, agape, search
my face, wandering around its edges.
She misjudges the cup, scalds
her right arm. My eyes must do that,

grapple for a focal point like a twirling
ballerina. I've memorized my kitchen
by its form: the coffee pot next to
the good outlet, oil and vinegar
on the stovetop. My fear begins here:

in laundry baskets and playthings
my future may leave in the living room
without warning. Myopic, I will break
against small unknowns. I am trying
not to lose an inch of this world:

the gush of a bloody knee, the kneeling
of the sun come evening, the face
of a son to come in five years
when I will see less, but enough
to know what parts of me he bears.

Straw Into Gold

I.
In another state, Mom's wiping down the glass case
of a bakery display, surprised to find herself past fifty

and returning to her first job—at fifteen she rose early
to ready doughnuts and this readying was supposed

to end with marriage or childbirth or some other thing
she did correctly. She always nodded when the dog barked

at her own image in the sliding glass door. She calls
to tell me I would like the anise cookies the baker makes

on Wednesdays, that she likes them even though
she doesn't like anise—something about delicacy

and balance. I tell her I am baking a pie because
I have company and she sighs relieved that I have

company or that I am capable of the kind of care
that it takes to bake a pie. She reminds me

to chill the crust dough until it doesn't stick,
to slice the apples thin and not use too much sugar,

as if I didn't own a collection of frilly aprons
she'd sewn. As if I wasn't raised better.

II.

In early dusk Michigan tries
to call, but I turn my phone off
to not hear my mother,
who is not wearing the red dress
we both like, the one
I borrowed for a dance,
Valentine's Day. I was alone
but pretty, thin legs trying
to be graceful in pumps,
or was it sex trying to be
seen? But I want to
see her in it, her face
clear. In a family portrait
my aunt who's good with photos
took, Mom's in a red dress
and her eyes are bright
but nervous. For the lights?
Or what I could do to ruin
the shot, my heavy squirm
trying to escape her
lap? I want us both to be
our youth selves when they said
we were bright and looked like
girls who would marry
well, despite our families,
which we are to each other.

III.
Mom's trying to prove that motion lessens
dread. Her hands
are perpetually doing—shoveling ash
from the woodstove,
threading the night through an embroidery needle.
The holidays have made me
a boarder again in her home, ungrateful deserter,
beastly mirror of
her twenties. She comes to me with wine
and says she needs me
to teach her bravery. I imagine her young and dancing,
delirious, unflinching. How
she must have worn her vices like sequins and discoed
her body new. She tells me her name
means an inquisition. Women she hasn't seen since the eighties,
since she moved to this city,
say her maiden name, say she looks good, the years good
to her face, unblemished—
and always ask, dulcet as housecats, *Wasn't it your brother*
who killed that boy? The cashier,
dead again. The gun reloaded. Drugs pirating her brother's
veins. The trigger, the body. *Is he still in prison? Still*
alive? I tell her we can change
what her name means. In a better version of this life
her name means maker
of beautiful garments, her name means all the warmth
she's quilted carefully out of scraps.

Amends

In a better version of this life, I think we could
sit at the same table, maybe
in Minneapolis, where I first met your wife
in a college bar and drank sangria
until my lips turned purple (which isn't
a very long time, really). I'd like
to speak in low, sweet tones like families do
on television to denote a closeness—
that's like when we slept
in bunk beds, and I'd listen for your breath
to decelerate into the wandering
mind of night. I'm afraid
I have sold our childhoods for less
than a loaf of bread. I still dream
of crashing cars that I never learned
how to drive. Sometimes I find you
in the trunk and you tell me
not to throttle us into
another police chase. How to explain
duplicity? When I tried to walk
out of the sorrow that rendered me
a household incubus,
the shards I'd made of love
gouged deep into my calloused heels.
After desperate, there is
a humming prayer that hangs
in the dense air:
The horizon means love without
end. And so it is.

I am trying to build a church
out of this life
that you'd like to visit: I'll prepare
a communion of
snicker-doodles and Diet Coke.
Please save room.

A Beige House on Jolly Road

Enough space for privacy, Dad's stereo,
Mom's garden, kids, even my rowdy dog
and make-believe: it was a fine house
for a family. Empty forties littered ditches
on either side of the long gravel drive,
but two acres of woods kept us separate
from old Caddies next to trailers, wangstas,
the McDonald's shut down for vending
more than criminally unhealthy burgers,
the dollar store that reeked of diapers
and burnt rubber, the Rite Aid shoplifted
into empty shelves and slumped guards.
It was a fine house. The man with the pail
full of knives and rusted garden tools
taking up fort in the front flower bed
must have thought so. In one version,
the gold in his teeth snarled at us,
my brother and I, as we raced up the drive,
chubby legs leaping over mud puddles.
My brother studied him, silently fished
the house key from his backpack,
unlocked the door and locked us back in.
In another version, it was summer,
and we'd been sent out to weed beans
or play save the princess and came running
back inside to tell Mom there was a man,
a stranger, danger, a pail full of knives
to carve us into ghosts if he wanted.
He never did. The cops came hours later

and recognized him. There were handcuffs.
He was real as the hostas and pink impatiens
he crouched amongst: I imagine he chose that bed
for the shade of the nearby maple reaching
over the roof. It was a fine house.

Epithalamion

Before the shivered coast of Lake Michigan
I know and love the least: Holland, Dutch Calvinist
settled land of chaste tulips and guns galore—
Before my family and an officiating man of God
(a Unity reverend who loves a man
in a natural truth that is not sanctified
by the courts in this state, a man
my father has voted may not wed
his own love under this particular sky)—
Before the bride-to-be's tearful family and God—
My brother vows to keep loving a woman
I don't know as well as my hairstylist
but watched step nearly nude
into a diamond-white, corseted construct
her sisters and mother maneuvered
into an elegant silhouette around her.
And she vows, too, to love
my brother, whom I know less now
than when we were busy building forts
out of God's good leftovers,
than when I knew he loved my living
enough to frighten off high school suitors
who dared swoop in on his one charge.
As they kiss in the name of belonging
to one another, my last hoarded feather,
my joy wafts southward down the shore
toward the loud lonely of Chicago,
where I thought I might marry once.
If I were better at keeping love

where it is needed, I might have
pinned the molted, dun-colored thing
to my cropped hair. If I were better
at loving when it is needed,
I might have asked the wind
to quiet its frigid so I could concentrate
on my brother's big eyes
when they sighted his bride coming
to take his offering of home.

The Saddest Thing

Was it more like wearing Grandpa Gordon's MSU
sweatshirt to bed seven years after his death or dust-
ing the banister of his home for the last smudges of his
stroke-trembled hand? More like knowing the sweatshirt
was the last gift I gave him or remembering he pulled me
aside that Christmas to say how proud he was that I'd
gotten into college? More like the slick of ice beside the
mailbox crashing the fragile old man's brain against the
paved drive. More like blood too thinned by Coumadin
to clot. More like the pillow of blood his wife of fifty-five
years found him resting upon. Like the hospital room. Like
reading Dylan Thomas to his son, my dad, as if it could
solve what doctors couldn't. The saddest thing, it was the
last night he breathed: When we sent Grandma home to
rest, she kissed his quiet brow and said, *Goodbye Honey.*
Her eyes wouldn't leave his body as she left: That look.

Fragile Globes

O serotonin flood,
if I can only know one god, please
let it be you.
Three fathoms deep in your swishing,
I have loved
a stranger's freckled boy
blowing soap bubbles at a kitten on the sidewalk.
I have loved the animal
batting her mitts at the clear, fragile globes.
I have loved the winter air,
the inclined road, the knocking of a shoulder bag
against my right side.
Oh, I know, it was human and good
to ask the boy the kitten's name
and wave at his mother who was waving
and pretty in her snow coat.
Your absence is always a bad face to show
the world that is tired
of bad faces. Is there a right side
to happiness? It is human
to be ruled by chemical and synapse.
It is good to live
unmolested by the glowering horizon.
I do not want to skulk
through fluorescent corridors of academia
and forget to love the quiet
pointed bulbs of gladiolas
readying themselves to be beautiful
in August for all of us. In the photo

of my grandmother in her crisp satin
wedding dress, it is August
and she is grinning over an armload
of gladiolas, and I am glad
they are there for her.
I am glad I was held in those arms,
adored like that.
I want to adore the world,
to drink my ginger tea and grin
at every gentle thing I have known
and will know.

Goodbye to the Poetics of Recklessness

O decade of recklessness,
of rumble strips and close calls,
I am leaving you in the bright
stabby dawn of January.
Your sick body of grief stroked
my bleached straw hair
and it wasn't the same as want
but smelled like it—
cigarettes and aftershave
for days sleeping till noon
but not alone.
The repeated movement
got a little arthritic
toward the end.
The only voice left in me
said *that's enough!*
and meant it. The grace
tremor between skewering
myself on the guardrail
and going on living
was getting too slight.
You can keep my dowry
of wine bottles, keep
every death you've hoarded
in me. I don't need
your gaudy chandeliers of
just one more time.
I can close my eyes
and be filled with light.

Spell for Rachel's Eightieth Birthday

Four decades of sage smudging apartments of five children grown
into their kingdoms.

Three of your thick grey hairs, each the length of a toddler,
left on a pillowcase in my guest bedroom
where fate or mischief has carved your initials into the crown molding.

An unpoliced pink sky.
A rosewood wand carved by your love.
A trip to the moon on a spaceship named Loretta.

The reincarnation of Amy Winehouse.
New joy songs tattooed on our feet.
A piñata for every occasion.
An occasion for every pair of dancing shoes.
Ice for every swollen cankle.

Salted caramel everything. Everything we want
on sale at Wegmans. Free samples of brie and cannolis.

Enough time to bitch about our bones over mimosas and migas.
Enough time to paint our nails black and fill vases with lilacs.

Enough.

Soft clothes of ghosts
who are not us.

Not Gently Will I Lose Her

For if she were to die, my one, the only Michigan anchor
steadying me in this erudite mess of neologisms
for old truths, this university on a steep gorgeous hill
where we are funded generously to learn
to call our home-hearts trash, to discard them
on the curb for removal or vermin feasting—

If she were to die here as I nearly did in the winter
that did not lack light any more than the Midwest but did
swallow fierce the horizon, my peasant accent, wardrobe,
fifth after fifth of *please, muscles, raise me back into want*—

If I were to find her gone and going away from
me, from her body, if there were blood in her mouth
or shat panties or a neck lynched and swaying
or a note or a thousand other agonies—

> I should roar at the many beasts in this landscape,
> pull my hair out strand by strand until I am a sight
> for sorry eyes, carve her name into every tree
> with a butcher knife.
>
> &
>
> I should cradle whatever is left of her cold head
> in my hands and cry out to the God I don't have:
> *No, not this one. You give her back.*
>
> &
>
> I should gouge out my eyes, hack off the first hand
> that touched death and wander the gorges
> searching for a force to finish the job.

&
I should weep a sixth Great Lake to drown in.

Which is to say that I need
with all my flesh & wonder
for you to survive.

Scheherazade

In this story we are old and proud
in our slack skin and one-pieces
on a rock coast of Chicago.
With our gray hair, we are elegant
animals gathering light.
You are telling me stories
about your dead
who are not us, not now—
a love taken by cancer,
who left you wintered by grief
for two summers
that are not this one.
The wind is in love with us,
keeps teasing pages
of books written to soothe
the most feral debts we carry.
You are laughing loud
because it is good
for the lungs to laugh loud.
The years we cashed
playing chicken with our bodies
and time, licking whiskey
off our elbows until we collapsed
into welcome mats,
never repossessed our names.
We are old enough to know to be good
to our working lungs, our working
legs, our working hearts,
which have delivered us here,
to this beach, this city,
this thinning side of happiness.

Stevie Edwards is a poet, editor, educator, and an advocate for mental health awareness. She is currently Editor-in-Chief at *Muzzle Magazine*, Acquisitions Editor at YesYes Books, and a Lecturer at Cornell University. Her first book, *Good Grief* (Write Bloody 2012), won an open manuscript contest and received two post-publication awards, the Independent Publisher Book Awards Bronze in Poetry and the Devil's Kitchen Reading Award from Southern Illinois University - Carbondale. Her poems have appeared in *Verse Daily, Rattle, Devil's Lake, Indiana Review, Salt Hill, We Will be Shelter: Poems for Survival,* and elsewhere. She holds an MFA in creative writing from Cornell University and a BA in economics and English from Albion College.

Notes

"Fiat Lux" observes "The weird, wonderful world of bioluminescence," a TedTalk by Edith Widder.

"Daily Weather: 2013" borrows the line "the landscape listens" from Emily Dickinson.

The title "Naming What Is Lost, What Remains" is the ultimate line of "At Thirty" by Lynda Hull.

Acknowledgments

These poems have appeared in the following journal and anthologies (some under different titles):

Amethyst Arsenic–"Goodbye to the Poetics of Recklessness"
A-Minor Magazine–"Double Survivor" and "Preface to
Eating the Night Whole"
The Bakery–"Twirling the Darkness in a Holiday Inn,"
"Come Ye Faithful Savior Man," and "Good Vision"
Birdfeast–"Genesis of the Only Michigander Who Doesn't
Drive" and "A Beige House on Jolly Road"
BODY–"Protest"
Devil's Lake–"Against Ghosts"
Drunk in a Midnight Choir–"Long Distance Aubade" and
"What Was the Most Delicate Thing in the Psych Ward?"
Gesture–"Offering," "Take as Needed," "I Keep Trying to
Functional," "Waiting in Line at the Temp Agency," and
"Post-Theist Logic"
Heart–"Straw Into Gold"
Juked–"Stepping Inside of November"
Likewise Folio–"The Beast"
NAILED–"Luck, Luck, Noose;" "Menstruation at Twenty-
Six," and "This is just to say…"
Paper Darts–"First Move After the Year of Hangings"
PANK–"A Lusting" and "Manners"
Pine Hills Review–"Dear Critic,"
Radius–"Revisionist History"
Revolution House–"Hush Now," and "Naming What Is Lost,
What Remains"
Salt Hill–"Fiat Lux"

Solstice–"In the Psych Ward"
Southern Indiana Review–"Pretty Death Myths I: Gorge"
Stone Highway Review–"Pretty Death Myths II: Steering Wheel"
Stonecoast Review–"To Houdini," and "Overrun"
Sweet: A Literary Confection–"Thanksgiving" and "Not Gently Will I Lose Her"
The Adroit Journal–"Lament With Rhinestones and Wonder," and "Scheherazade"
Thrush Poetry Journal–"We Were Trying to Write a Love Story," "The Diplomat," and "A Blessing"
Used Furniture Review–"Witch and Dirty Wardrobe"
Vinyl Poetry–"Fabulousness"
We Will Be Shelter–"Fragile Globes"
Word Riot–"Humanly"

*Some poems previously appeared in chapbooks: *Atomic Girl* (Tired Hearts Press, 2014) and *little bones* (Thoughtcrime Press, 2013). Drafts of several poems also appeared in the Tupelo Press 30/30 Project in September 2013.

Thank you to Carrie Seitzinger for wanting to bring this book into the world. Thank you to Kendra DeColo, Jeanann Verlee, KMA Sullivan, Lyrae Van Clief-Stefanon, Ishion Hutchinson, and Sean Patrick Mulroy for their valuable feedback on the many drafts of *Humanly*. Thank you to Benjamin Clark, Aricka Foreman, Emily O'Neill, Alice Fulton, Rachel McKibbens, and Jacob Rakovan for helping me to revise various poems in this collection. Thanks to the McKibbens-Rakovan family for opening their home to me again and again: this manuscript would never have been finished if not for Jacob's beef arepas, Rachel's cackle, and the aggregate hugs of their children. Thank you to my friends and family in Chicago and Michigan who still keep a light on for me. Thank you to the Women of Pink Door for helping me to believe in this project, myself, life, poetry, etc.

The Homeboy Songs is Robert Lashley's complex homage to the black community of Tacoma, Washington. As part of a Northwest population with people from the deep South and a survivor of the Hilltop gang wars of the early 90s, Lashley's poetry makes sense of the multitude of voices that have surrounded him over the years. His passion joins high lyric poetry burnished by narrative structure, with a language attuned to the ear and the complexities of the human voice.

the homeboy songs

robert
lashley

The Homeboy Songs
poems by **Robert Lashley**

$14.95 | 102 pages | 5.5" × 8.5" | softcover | ISBN: 978-0-9848744-7-7

"Robert Lashley is not just playing with a full deck; he's playing with all the goddamn decks. He trades in Shakespeare and Simone, Yeats and Dove, Auden and Three 6 Mafia and razzles and hymns, all with the kind of swagger and strut that asks and offers no apology. *The Homeboy Songs* is a stunning achievement, announcing Lashley not just as an important poetic voice, but as a new kind of prophet, one offering vivid visions not of the future, but of the vast sparkling Now. His poems are charged and smart and smarting; they seduce and hiss; they are, above all, incredibly potent, and incredibly necessary. Look, they say. This is how to look directly into the sun without going blind. This is how to live without flinching.

—**MINDY NETTIFEE**, author of *Rise of the Trust Fall* and *Glitter in the Blood*

"Whether on-stage or on-the-page, Robert Lashley's poems are about voice. His is a sophisticated voice driven by passion, and supported by both intellect and structure. Few poets can equal the power and originality of *The Homeboy Songs*."

—**JAMES BERTOLINO**, author of *Every Wound Has A Rhythm*

Jacob Rakovan's *The Devil's Radio* broadcasts the elegies of so many, in a voice that lies down with them in their graves, touches their bones, and knows their stories. Cast against a backdrop of Appalachia in exile, Rakovan's collection of poems mines the dark veins of life, love, and death.

The Devil's Radio
poems by **Jacob Rakovan**

$14.95 | 90 pages | 5.5" × 8.5" | softcover | ISBN: 978-0-9848744-4-6

'Urgently tender and elegiac, *The Devil's Radio* not only howls and hurts good, but also sings toward healing with a persistence that is life-affirming and devotional. With language and music that are oak-aged in exile and the deeply felt memory of Appalachia, these poems burn deliciously and relentlessly through the body and mind. Faced with the impossible wreckage of loss, of death after death, of trying to be a good man and father while staring down the thieving threat of graves, Rakovan employs a fairytale-like logic to reinvent elegy, to make sense of the senseless, to knock the grinning face off that 'sonofabitch' death and give the dead and living back their wonder.'

—**Stevie Edwards**, author of *Good Grief*

'American ghosts have to make up a song to sing as they weave their flight through our ruins—rural and industrial both. Few people care to listen to the horror and beauty of that chorus. In his debut collection, however, Rakovan tunes into this awesome and terrible ruckus, crafts for us a gothic ballad and rust-blade curse, the psalm plugged into a banged up tweed amp, elegy after elegy, eros, tenderness, fable and praise. After centuries of private wreckage and public forgetting, there is a poet composing something to make sense of it all and the sounds are playing on *The Devil's Radio*.'

—**Patrick Rosal**, author of *My American Kundiman* and
Uprock, Headspin, Scramble and Dive

Into the Dark & Emptying Field is
an interrogation of loneliness
and its many masks. It explores
innocence as the price of knowledge
in a host of voices that share an
emotional truth. McKibbens offers
a monument of understanding for
even the bleakest pieces of our
human conundrum.

Into the Dark & Emptying Field
poems by **Rachel McKibbens**

$14.95 | 88 pages | 5.5" × 8.5" | softcover | ISBN: 978-0-9848744-3-9

"Hard and as real as the ax blade, the poems in *Into the Dark & Emptying Field* are unapologeticall
fierce and undeniably gorgeous. Strikingly imaginative and expertly crafted, these necessar
poems shine a dubious flashlight on both the menace and the marvel that surrounds u
Otherworldly and at times shockingly brutal, McKibbens' work is both crucial and addictive.

—**Ada Limó**

"Rachel McKibbens' work shatters me and my world, then pieces us back together on the pag
like no other poetry I have ever read, creating a new reality, a self that feels what I cannc
feel, sees what I cannot see. These poems are at once dreamscapes and yet as solid and re
as stones in my hands, stones I want to press against my chest forever, then hurl back int
the infinity of space where words of such beauty and power surely come from."

—**Richard Blanc**

"The ancient Japanese swordsmiths categorized a sword by how many body parts it coul
pass through, i.e., a two-neck sword, a three-arm sword...The strongest and deadliest was
four-torso sword. This book is a four-torso sword. You will feel it, hard."

—**Jennifer L. Kno**

Carrie Seitzinger's
Fall Ill Medicine dwells in the
body, where memories gather
in full color, darkness waits in
our deepest feeling trials, and
frailties give way to strength.
Each poem offers the reader
a chance to remember, an
opportunity to forget, and a
reason to consider the things
that make us fragile humans.

Fall Ill Medicine
poems by **Carrie Seitzinger**

$10.95 | 88 pages | 5.06" × 7.81" | softcover | ISBN: 978-0-9848744-1-5

"In Carrie Seitzinger's collection *Fall Ill Medicine* we are healed. Seitzinger is a doctor of the
lyric moment, a humanist of narrative, and had the bedside manner any poet would be
lucky to have—that is a verse with truth, mystery, and kinetic energy. As she writes in her
poem "Freefall Flight," 'Then I walk to the window and fall out. / And it is beautiful and I
am happy.' And so we are lucky to walk into the windows of her poems, and through the fall
made beautiful and happy."

—**Matthew Dickman**
author of ***All-American Poem** & **Mayakovsky's Revolver: Poems***

"*Fall Ill Medicine* is a book poems that brings one back to body's story—with a brutal pull soft
as moth's wings. There is a love story that exists between objects and silences and ribs. There
is a lifestory that makes strength from our frailties. Carrie Seitzinger sings the body home."

—**Lidia Yuknavitch**
author of ***The Chronology of Water** & **Dora: A Headcase***

SMALL DOGGIES PRESS

Artful Fiction & Poetry
For Lovers of the Written Word

⟡

Small Doggies Press supports, defends, and publishes the most beautiful, challenging, and artful prose and poetry that we can find. We believe that the author has all the power, and our job is to create a context within which they, and most importantly their work, can flourish and find the intelligent, curious readership that it deserves.

Small Doggies Press is a division of Small Doggies Omnimedia, LLC, an Oregon. Corp.

Visit Us Today:

www.smalldoggiespress.com

CPSIA information can be obtained at www.ICGtesting.com
Printed in the USA
BVOW04n0455110315

391157BV00001B/1/P